EXPERT FINANCIAL ANALYSIS

EXPERT FINANCIAL ANALYSIS

ROWAN EVERHART

CONTENTS

1 Introduction to Financial Analysis   1

2 II. Tools and Techniques in Financial Analysis   5

3 III. Financial Statement Analysis   9

4 IV. Industry and Company Analysis   15

5 V. Forecasting and Valuation   19

6 VI. Risk Management and Mitigation   23

7 VII. Ethics and Professional Standards in Financia   27

8 VIII. Career Development in Financial Analysis   29

9 IX. Conclusion and Future Trends   35

Copyright © 2024 by Rowan Everhart
All rights reserved. No part of this book may be reproduced in any manner
whatsoever without written permission except in the case of brief quota-
tions embodied in critical articles and reviews.
First Printing, 2024

CHAPTER 1

Introduction to Financial Analysis

This book spotlights important findings for anyone embarking on a career as a financial analyst and for financial educators who design curricula to prepare students for a career in this field. The material presented in this book can help the professional student understand the motives behind the technical courses he or she must take and how that material fits into the overall scheme of working as a financial analyst. The material also informs the student and faculty of where, somewhat specifically, to concentrate their job search research and recruiting activities. Most importantly, the overview provides a very practical look at what it takes to be a successful financial analyst.

The bulk of the book consists of practical findings that are presented in five distinct sections. Other practical insights in the book include the topics that financial analysts believe their curricula should emphasize, the importance of communication skills in the eyes of hiring agents, the positive learning experiences of more recent graduates, and the material that employers believe is essential for students to learn. With the exception of this introduction and a list of references at the conclusion, the book is a brief three pages. The sections of the overview were derived from personal interviews with successful financial analysts who hold decision-making positions in their companies. The following topics will be explored in greater detail in each of the sections.

A. Definition and Importance of Financial Analysis

According to Beardsley, "Finance is basically defined as the management of money and encompasses activities such as investing, borrowing, lending, budgeting, saving, and forecasting. It is the art of creating and managing wealth. The behavior of a firm is also determined by the financing and investment activities of the organization. Financial management is the area of management dealing with the managers' decision on investing, financing, and returns. Financial analysis offers a base for taking rational decisions. It can present a faster, consistent, and increasingly perceptive definition of a firm and its issue of its development over time than management alone."

In today's competitive landscape, businesses have to generate top returns for their shareholders. Such expectations include the manager not only fulfilling investors' expectations but also making sound decisions and giving feasible suggestions. Such financial judgment influenced by past experience, intuition, and the worth approach are indispensable, but they should also be supported by partly scientific and quantitative scrutiny that is considered financial investigation. Financial analysis provides concrete economic data and clarity concerning the economics of the corporate company so company alumni can use corporate information to make corporate choices. Although the main role of financial analysis is fact-finding, it is as well broadly used for exploration and estimation.

B. Key Concepts and Terminology

Financial analysis is a highly quantitative and sometimes highly technical occupation. To engage in such analysis, the serious professional must become familiar with the specialized jargon of the profession, learning the precise definitions ascribed to a host of commonly used words and phrases. The ten key concepts of this text are as follows:

• Whenever someone considers the relative worth of something, be it a tangible asset or investment, or a set of numbers purported to describe and quantify the activities of a business entity, that person is applying the principles of financial analysis. These principles are not simply monetary in nature, focusing upon the determination of a factor or factors related to some form of financial gain. They are, far more broadly, the determination of worth, put forth in a host of dimensions and variations. Thus, one person can do a comprehensive written business analysis comparing several companies and suggesting one for investment in a long-term strategy, calling it "security analysis." Another person can do a quick "back-of-the-envelope" number-crunching to see if the investment of their capital in a single company is sound. Both are financial analysts.

• We will have to consider time-based elements in most of the analyses we do, such as dealing with different forms of money expense in the Simple Financial Statement Analysis. Further, since we use them in every facet of finances and investing, we will introduce them in later chapters to use in our discounted cash flow analyses.

II. Tools and Techniques in Financial Analysis

There are numerous different tools and techniques used in the realm of financial analysis. Some are quantitative while others are qualitative. The arriving at an interpretation of financial reports is generally not based on one method, but rather a combination. This section gives an overview of the types of analysis methods, both quantitative and qualitative, used to help financial analysts study and come to conclusions regarding private companies based on their financial information.

A financial analysis is the process of identifying the financial strengths and weaknesses of the firm by properly establishing relationships between the items of the balance sheet and the profit and loss account. Financial analysis provides, of course, only a broad outline of the firm's position. The results have to be interpreted in the best possible manner for the decision-makers. If an analysis is to be well done, the financial statements alone are not enough. Indeed, even as regards the annual financial statements, certain reservations have to be expressed. In fact, legal and management policies are open to manipulation. For example, the depreciation policy will affect the Profit and Loss statement. To assess how far the figures may be relied upon, it is necessary to verify the methods of establishing liabilities such as provisions.

A. Ratio Analysis

Financial analysts often use ratio analysis as a technique to evaluate a company's performance and prognosis. Ratios are mathematical results for important financial variables and successful relationships between them. Ratios help a financial analyst to examine the extent of profitability of a company, its weakness, efficiency, qualifications, profitability, and performance of its stakeholders. They also serve the auditor and the market by devising policies and investing decisions. Two main viewpoints on which ratios are sought in financial analysis are profitability ratios and investment ratios.

The profit ratios demonstrate the company's competitive advantages and are, therefore, the most critical ratios considered by the investors or the stockholders. Furthermore, unlike liquidity ratios, lenders like a high profitability that ensures the company's ability to meet its debt commitments and also the interest and principal payments. The main point of financial analysis is the evaluation of different ratios. To assure that the firm has the highest leverage and returns, we have to compare our performance with the other companies for the industry. Even if the firm is able to sell a product at a loss, it may be worthwhile to invest when it finds that its market is capable of handling a higher price during the future. To quantify just how much we can sell without loss (also called the margin of safety), it uses various ratios.

B. Cash Flow Analysis

The accurate calculation, analysis, and interpretation of cash flows are a vital part of any professional financial analysis. The lifeblood of any company is the cash they generate. The company can't write checks, purchase raw materials, or afford labor unless the cash is available. The accountant's team focuses heavily on the income statement and balance sheet, with much of the information on cash flows derived from changes on these two statements. There isn't any doubt, though, financial managers place the ultimate emphasis on cash flows because they are the most important element of the financial statements. Lots of perfectly nice firms go bankrupt because they run out of cash!

There are numerous reasons why a financial manager would be interested in the patterns of cash flows: They want to predict future cash flows to assist in planning - including budgeting, investment, and financing. They are getting paid according to cash flows, lenders always want their interest and repayments on a timely basis, regardless of how well or how bad the company is doing (unlike stockholders, who are at the bottom of the payment structure). They are interested in the company's ability to satisfy financial covenants (notably, Debt Coverage Service Requirements), as agreed upon in a loan contract. Just because you were in compliance at the signing of the loan does not mean you still are! They are apprehensive about a lack of liquidity for their short-term investors. There is a legitimate concern about a bad situation becoming worse (do you have enough cash to pay the bills? 3, 6, 9 months or more from now?). The relationships they have with their suppliers, especially when negotiating a line of credit.

C. Trend Analysis

The owner of Minnetonka Surplus & Equipment, who has been in business in the Minneapolis/St. Paul area for decades, once stated that the "best merchandise in the world will not sell above what we feel is the possible growing value." What is it that suggests that merchandise has "possible growing value?" The answer is trend. Trend consists of points spaced on a graph that follows such factors (allegedly) as economics, weather, fashion, peak seasons, industry happenings, and market ups and downs. The idea is that investors with this information can predict a future trend, probably something that costs less for the investor today than what it will be worth when sold later, for example in a month, a quarter, a year, or five or ten years. If the investor guesses wrong, there is the opposite trend (probability) in view, reducing considerable loss. There is no crystal ball; but critical, over time the occasional investment will increase in value.

A wise trend follower is interested in past value points and relies on a variety of methods based on facts. One of them is the use of trend lines. Another is the linear-trend line—what can develop, and does, from the value points that lie roughly between the upper and lower-limit bands of the regression-trend lines. Out of all the trend-line methods mentioned in Section V, the one Minnetonka recommends is the moving trend line. The spatial space distance between the upper and lower moving trend lines determines "a possible margin of safety" over time against loss.

III. Financial Statement Analysis

One of the critical subjects that help in financial analysis is financial statement analysis. Financial statement analysis consists of three words which require its description:

1. Financial 2. Statement 3. Analysis.

'Financial' refers to cash, fund, capital, and etc. 'Statements' refers to records, reports, documents, and etc. 'Analysis' refers to evaluation, conclusion, finding, interpretation, judgment, and etc. So, financial statement analysis refers to a study to assess the feasibility, stability, and profitability of a business entity. It enables to know the financial performance of the enterprise. Rules, conventions, and techniques remain the same despite these statements being in cash or fund. There are different types of financial statements such as the trading account, profit and loss account, balance sheet, and statement of changes in financial position of a business entity. These financial statements are to be prepared under accounting standard and to be presented in the annual report.

However, it is pertinent to describe who are the users of the financial reports, so that the users of the financial statements can analyze and make decisions: Investors and Their Advisers, Credit

Analysts and Bankers, Managers, Business Owners and Other Employees, Regulatory Organizations and Governments, Employees/Labor Unions, Financial Advisors, Customers, and Suppliers. In general, the financial analysts rely upon financial analysis to decide whether to invest in a particular company, assess the qualitative factors, assess the risks, as well as measure the value of a company. Financial analysis requires financial statement of a business entity to interpret and analyze. The financial statement analysis is an important part of the comprehensive financial analysis in every business.

3.1. A. Balance Sheet Analysis

Analyzing the financial statements of an enterprise involves dealing with financial statements. One of the most significant and insightful financial statements is the balance sheet, also referred to as the statement of financial position. The balance sheet generally reflects the financial position of an enterprise at the end of an accounting period. It shows what an entity owner's financial interest is in an enterprise and what the enterprise owns and owes. Three important components of financial statements are owners' equity, assets, and liabilities. Analysis of each one of them includes horizontal, cross-sectional, and common-size analysis.

In this section, the major analysis of balance sheet items and ratios include:

Liquidity: Ability to meet short-term obligations is ensured by the entity's liquidity. Therefore, analysis of these factors enables a user of financial statements to comment on the ability of an enterprise to meet its short-term obligations.

Solvency: This is less concerned with short-term liquidity, but more concerned with the ability of its assets during a longer period of time. Therefore, this ratio shows the strength of an enterprise.

Section 1 will focus on balance sheet analysis in a lawful manner. Through a balance sheet, experts can identify solvency and liquidity of a company which are as follows:

1. Solvency refers to the ability of a company to pay its long-term obligations when they become due. A business, increasing or, for some time, maintaining its investment in non-current assets, risks that this investment may prove unremunerative and lead to the business's insolvency.

2. Liquidity refers to the ability of a business to pay its short-term obligations as and when they fall due. The balance sheet in itself provides some information about the liquidity of a business by setting out the assets owned by it and the sources of the finance used for acquiring those assets, corresponding to the items listed in (3) and (4). Liquidity and solvency are mirror images.

B. Income Statement Analysis

The income statement presents the revenue and expense performance of a company over a specified period of time. Revenues recognized depend on the period of the completion and collection of the related cash. Expenses recognized depend on the associated benefits. There are many ways to analyze the information presented in the income statement, and the critical analyst must be able to work with and interpret the information at various levels of aggregation. Over the life of the firm, thousands of individual transactions are aggregated into financial statement components. So it is at this level that we can get our best information.

In general, analysts use the income statement alone for one of three strategic purposes. Using only the income statement, they assess the income-generating efficiency and effectiveness of a firm, highlight and evaluate managers' decisions to create and establish market share, or they use it to evaluate present and future business conditions. The income statement is typically used not in isolation but in conjunction with the other financial statements. In this situation, it is generally used to verify other financial findings or firm strategies. As will become obvious soon enough, the analyst who evaluates a company with only one of the financial statements is not being as thorough as they could be. The income statement plus the balance sheet form the basis of judicious financial analysis.

Income statement components include the entity's gross margin (which can be divided into the gross profit margin and the cost of goods sold ratio), general and selling expenses, accounts receivable analysis, profit margin analysis (which can be divided into the operating profit margin and the net profit analysis ratio), and disposal of assets component analysis. All of these components deal with the formal aspects of analyzing this kind of financial statement.

C. Cash Flow Statement Analysis

Part A of this book introduces the cash flow statement in general and addresses the three sections of the cash flow statement specifically. Whereas some investors and financial experts prefer to use the indirect method for creating cash flow statements, the direct method is closer to the interests of security analysts because it emphasizes the cash payments and receipts related to items in the income statement. A major part of the cash flow statement is the investigation of cash from operations. A large amount of cash from operations is clearly a very good sign, but achieving proper accounting rules should also be concerned with. Among direct cash flow from operating activities, there are good signs, such as producing cash from services suddenly. Meanwhile, it shows that cash comes from a deferral in accounts; this may show problems, then the advantages that might affect future years.

The cash flow statement does not gather and display the financial flow items. Moreover, four main distinctions in the figures between the cash flow statement and accounting numbers from the income statement or balance sheet are found: (1) accounting income contains figures on non-cash items (losses and incomes), income, and insurance expenses; (2) accounts include depreciation or replacement figures for purchases of new plants, as realized in the past years; and (3) accounts include the differences between anticipated and cash-paid taxes. While average investors can investigate financial statements, cash flow statements are also necessary for financial professionals. They need a much more comprehensive evaluation of a company's distinct activities, leading them to identify where circumstances and investments are based on forecast-cash production in the future.

IV. Industry and Company Analysis

As security analysts, we are striving to understand and value the securities in which we are considering. The companies, however, operate within industries, which are in turn sub-sectors of the larger economy. This section examines how subjecting an industry tier analysis of a sector is indispensable in order to develop an understanding of company performance or future prospects on either a standalone rather than relative basis. Even after studying company performance, the company analyst is inevitably confronted with industry issues, integrating his perspectives with those of the economist and the portfolio manager.

To approach the industry analysis, we will first look at the "macro" or broad-level picture in terms. In an effort to generate trading ideas, we cast our gaze across several sectors. The process begins with broad-level analysis in order to comprehend an industry segment in terms of revenue distribution, operating margins, share of competition, and customer concentration. However, recognizing and understanding the industry groupings and their individual segments is an absolutely necessary first step, without which an analyst cannot begin to properly analyze a company. Influencing many aspects of company performance and valuation, industry analysis is of utmost importance to those aspiring to increase the effectiveness and accuracy of any project or investment. Furthermore, industry analysts and investors need to recognize not only the quality of an industry but also the economics that may give rise to negative performance or declining profitability. Companies operate within industries, and therefore industry analysis provides important context for understanding and valuing companies.

A. Understanding Industry Dynamics

An industry is a group of homogeneous firms operating in the same line of business. Generally, an industry of concentrated pure situations contains few firms operating in the industry, and they control the majority of the market share. An industry of competitive pure situations consists of many firms, none of which have the ability to significantly influence market price or supply. Competent financial analysis of a firm can only be completed when the underlying industry dynamics are understood.

Market Trends The ease with which firms and industries can be analyzed is influenced by trends. Trends are long-run movements in economic behavior. They have three key characteristics: direction, consistency, and persistence. Breaks are points of significant change in established trends. When a break occurs, it is important to determine if it is temporary or permanent. Chartists are interested in identifying trend movements to predict future price behavior; however, trend movements can be used to interpret any variable, characteristic, or phenomenon in the economy.

Competitive Forces Economic entities are never completely free to act based on their own impulses. The forces emanating from the competitive process place constraints upon the behavior of individual firms. Some businesses face more stringent conditions than others, and part of the task of analysis is evaluating how competitive forces will act to influence firm results. Michael Porter identified five key factors or forces to consider:

- The threat of intensified existing competition - The threat of new entrants - The power of buyers - The power of suppliers - The threat of substitute products or services.

B. Company Performance Metrics

We have many options in assessing the financial health and operational efficiency of the companies. Many investors, bankers, and credit analysts, and company managers consider the income statement and balance sheet to be the two most important statements. The financial success or failure of a company is often measured by how much revenue or how few liabilities it can generate. Some widely used metrics include: the company's net income; earnings before interest, taxes, depreciation, and amortization (EBITDA); price-earnings ratio; return on equity, net income excluding interest expense and after-tax (i.e., NOPAT); free cash flows; and trends in sales, total assets, and capital expenditures.

Analysts and, if the company is publicly traded, the investing public often examine the returns generated by investing activities. For this reason, cash flow statements and footnotes are a good source of information. But the statement has shortcomings as an indicator of company performance. It may vary significantly due to changes in motor vehicle tag fees or property taxes payable, for example. Many profitable companies, in other words, may have very low or even negative net cash generation. Long-term liabilities, including bonds or notes, are other important aspects of a company's standing. Pending sales contraction, for instance, will force a firm to sell assets to repay liabilities. Accounts receivable are also measured as a ratio of sales to assess the financial flexibility implicit in the "plasticization" of earnings. Fixed asset turnover and depreciation expense are also frequently used in investment analysis.

V. Forecasting and Valuation

Forecasting is at the basis of financial analysis. We want to forecast revenues, investment outlays, cash flows, expenses, cost of capital, etc. This will enable us to estimate a firm's future profits and cash flows. Why do you think this is so important to a forecast? There are many different ways to do a forecast, most of them based on time series (or cross-sections) data. For example, we might use the past behavior of a variable to forecast its future (for this to work the past must be a good predictor of the future), information from experts or on other similar cases. We may also want to test for the accuracy of our forecasts. In addition, we would like to know: Does valuation really matter? Does it change? Can you forecast the change?

Investors make financial decisions only when they expect to earn returns greater than the costs of the firm's resources, including its intellectual resources. Analysts should be able to value an asset or a business to assess a financial opportunity and the risks associated with it. Some of the valuation methods that can be used are: free cash flow, price multiples, earnings/cash flow multiples, leveraged buyouts (LBO) analysis - these could be different ways for valuing an entire business. Approaches related to pricing claims on assets are the arbitrage pricing model, portfolio theory approach, and option pricing. A key aspect in the valuation analysis is risk. Valuation professionals are obsessed with risk, in particular with the factors that might change the risk (this is why forecasting is important). When selecting the discount rate to be applied in a traditional valuation model (one that uses as a fundamental cash flows or income statements instead of dividends) cash flows that are discounted (like in NPV) should be "discounted at a rate that reflects the risk inherent in those cash flows".

A. Forecasting Techniques

Forecasting techniques provide a way to predict future financial outcomes of companies. There are many techniques and models that have been developed over the years to aid in the financial forecasting process. The following paragraphs provide an overview of a few of the methods for forecasting. The company or analyst can use a single method or a combination of methods to forecast financial numbers.

Time-series analysis looks at only historic data. It is a flow of observations that represents the yield of a company over a number of periods. The time-series exercise is defined by the choice of two variables: the dependent variable (Y) (example: sales of a company) and the time period (e.g., yearly, monthly units). Points are arranged chronologically, and the relationship between X and Y is explained. A trend line can be added to the chart and, although the data may fluctuate on a monthly basis, the monthly data fluctuating above and below this trendline over time will have an average annual growth rate very close to the average annual growth rate based on yearly data. Preliminary forecasting of time series is beneficial. This is preliminary forecasting, but the procedure provides statistical values such as correlation coefficients, calculation of R squared, standard error of estimate, an independent variable, etc.

B. Valuation Methods

A main task of financial analysis is to determine the investment value of an asset or a company. "Investment value" is the value of future cash flows or of the right to receive future cash flows. There are different methods for this.

1. Net Asset Value From the point of view of company valuation, the NAV (also called book value) is the starting point for the calculations. It represents the total assets increase over the valuation period and is made up of: a. New cash flows (cash in/out) b. Net finance generated by operating activities c. Capital expenditure on fixed assets d. Both, decrease/increase in working capital. If costs are higher than profits, the NAV decreases and the company is worth less than it was at the start. The NAV is the excess of assets over external funds.

2. Separation of Value and Profitability In the course of a discussion of the value-based management approach, damages obtained for the DFC-method in expected warranty contracts are contrasted with claims which must be made good in administrative judicial appeal. Damages obtained have a price function referring to the expected generated hazard. The price function is based on the expected value of claim which he have to pay compared with the as-is state. Commonly, the expected value of claim is modeled by the expected HSIA-value of the compensation to be paid because of unhealthy effects. When using inquiry information to identify appropriate wage subsidies, the relevance of damaged loss of amenity and losses as are not reflected in price generally, financial analysis to infer more details about public available data which are matter of interest used to compare multiple different items yields a monetary value to those inflicted with them or better. It also converts the routine disengage-

ment of hazards context in economic terms. In the European Union and in some developing countries both economic financial and benefit cost assessment tend to be more quantitatively oriented.

VI. Risk Management and Mitigation

1. Types of financial risks: a. Business Risk b. Financial Risk c. Insolvency Risk d. Liquidity Risk e. Legal Risk f. Political Risk g. Operational Risk h. Price Risk i. Credit Risk j. Settlement Risk k. Country Risk l. Systematic Risk

2. Categories of Risk: a. Credit Risk: It reflects the probability of loss from defaults of the counterparty on the assets held by it. Credit risk includes both liquidity and price risks. b. Sovereign Risk: It arises from risk variables, which are not amenable to control by the corporate. It is generally associated with the incidence of financial crisis, war, and similar other macro variables. c. Systematic Risk: It reflects the probability of loss due to adverse market and economic developments that are common to all financial markets. d. Employee Life Cycle vs My Career

VI. Risk Management and Mitigation 3. Business Risk (Operating Risk): It reflects the profits being earned in the normal course of business. If a business is run efficiently, further analysis mainly focuses on assessing the financial and systematic risk. 4. Financial Risk: It reflects the profits on a business including borrowings. The objective of financial management is to attempt to maximize the profit while protecting the entity from the impact of systematic risk. The probability arising out of capital structure would involve a study of the amount of fixed cost or borrowing and the source of these funds. Optimum funding results only when the marginal cost of capital equals marginal gains out of funds. Financial analysis largely focuses on assessing the nature and quantum of financial and systematic risk. 5. Insolvency Risk: It reflects the probability of default on account of inability to meet the payment obligations in time due to a lack of financial resources. These arise primarily due to poorly worked-out borrowing programs and also the size of the borrowings made. 6. Liquidity Risk: It is also known as the marketability risk and reflects the probability of loss from the need to sell paper securities at a price lower than the anticipated normal yield, due to unanticipated advance and/or decrease in the interest rates. If a valid hedge already anticipates an extraordinary situation, then liquidity risk can, perhaps, be the least to be looked into. 7. Legal Risk: Corporates also confront the risk of loss due to the inability to enforce rights under the legally enforceable documents entered into by the counterparties. Clearly, a valid study on the status of legal enforceability should largely indicate the quantum of loss on this risk element. 8. Political Risk: It arises when operations are stretched across the border where loading, unloading, carrying, or similar other territorial operations need to be carried out. 9. Operational Risk: It reflects the probability of a loss stemming from the execution of an organizational process. It is usually conducted on a sector-by-sector basis and measures the size of operation-dependent events not operational losses that have affected the entity, thus establishing the probability of their happening in percentage terms. 10. Credit Risk: It reflects the probability of losses for reasons pertaining to the behavior of the counterparties with whom the exposure is taken. Such exposures usually reflect the uncertainty in counterparty default.

Thus, suitable classification of risk opens the scope of better risk assessment and control over the pace or quantum of loss. Financial management is largely focused on assessing the operational and financial risk and recommends the suitable strategies for controlling these risks in the long run.

A. Types of Financial Risk

Every business faces various kinds of financial risks when it operates. Understanding the nature of a risk can serve as a solid foundation for suggesting feasible techniques for assessing those levels of risk. In a similar vein, the risk management of any type of enterprise is expected to be particularly vigilant regarding those areas of risk that may pose monetary dangers on a greater level. Some important classifications of risk—pertinent for our discussion on the financial analysis of an organization—are:

Financial Business Risk b. Financial Risk of an Organization and Investor c. Non-Financial Business Risk

We can divide the financial business risk into two more general risk types:

Those business risks which impact the cash flows through the market influences like changing interest rate. b. The business risks which affect mostly through the firm or company results like determination of dividend amount. These risks are purely company-specific and have no association with the business's position regarding the market. An appropriately framed risk management process in accordance with the suggested tactics and techniques will be presented under the revised syllabus of CFAST, which will definitely be able to deliver the risk managers with very cost-effective practices for managing both the market as well as non-market associated risks. Moreover, the categorizations of risks under the proposed revision of revised risk management syllabus are based on the type of exposure which includes one foreign exchange rate and two interest rate as well as separately based on the market, credit, and operational associated risks only.

B. Risk Management Strategies

The role of financial analysts is to examine current and past data, to evaluate sectors, industries, and companies in those sectors, and to estimate the rate of return that investors can expect. To accomplish this, analysts must also estimate the riskiness of the prospective investments. In this chapter, we explore various ways to manage financial risk in order to gain higher returns. By understanding these risk management approaches, it will also provide some insight into financial analysis practices because the identification and communication of risk with investors is an important duty of many financial analysts.

The purpose of this part is to discuss the various ways available to a person who would like to manage financial risk. The strategies are long insurance, short insurance, self-insurance, termination, risk-sensitive spending or investment practices, and diversification. In discussing the strategies, we would also want to provide some information about how the person could go about implementing the strategy. For instance, how does one attain self-insurance or diversification and what are some advantages or disadvantages to these strategies. While it is not required, it would be beneficial to speculate as to whether these strategies would be available to or easily implemented by large versus small corporations or individuals. Transitioning to the next part, we might provide some ideas for integrating these risk management strategies choice into the risk assessment portion of a financial analysis.

VII. Ethics and Professional Standards in Financia

Professional ethics are a guide to help guide one when in doubt, in situations that in many cases have no clear right or wrong. They are also a foundation of public trust in the practice of any profession. In the realm of financial analysis, there are a few important guidelines that vary somewhat from country to country, but by and large have a lot in common. One of the most fundamental professionals on all of these lists is integrity. Maybe the official definition is a little too legal/controversy driven, but the ethical definition of integrity touches a little more closely to the definition required of financial analysts. The CFA Institute states that CFA charter-holders' behavior must take the form of honest communication, subordination of personal advantage to clients, and avoidance of conflicts of interest. Just as other professionals should act in the best interest of their clients, so should financial analysts.

In the United States, an act and the following regulatory rules make up the bulk of the regulations to which financial analysts must adhere. Generally, the code of standards that financial analysts should be in possession of lists the most important ethical principles, which in many cases, also are the first ones listed in an individual user's pathfinder, or the first section of an industry analysis paper. These fundamental considerations are thus at the fore of the profession and market information. These foundations are listed in the figure below and are comparable with any set of standards.

A. Code of Ethics for Financial Analysts

A. Code of Ethics for Financial Analysts. The code for professional standards issued by the CFA Institute also applies. The CFA Institute Code of Ethics establishes the ethical principles to apply to all investment and financial professionals. The profession as a whole benefits from the ethical behavior of all members. Treating all professionals with respect and fairness allows us to be team players and helps us to excel in our dealings with the investing community. Professional analysts demonstrate their respect for the profession by being accountable for their actions.

1. Integrity: Investors must have trust to function. By adhering to this standard and applying ethical principles, we shall be able to contribute to the development of the profession. We comply with regulations, processes, and requirements relevant to our conduct as professionals. We will not engage in any action that will discredit the profession. 2. Objectivity and Independence: The Equity Analyst must maintain intellectual honesty and objectivity in their research. To ensure that the research report is not influenced inappropriately by either the bank's banking intention or by its supervisory agreement, the sponsor requirement rule is supposed to help. This relationship would be revealed through the disclosure of the bank's advisory relationships and/or investment banking relationships with, and an investment in, the company, by the apparent analyst(s) involved. Our research should be created and supported with a thorough and unbiased examination of the facts.

VIII. Career Development in Financial Analysis

Financial analysis is one of the best-represented business-related careers in the world, and students and employees interested in this field can take many paths in numerous fields. The question of "how to get a job in financial analysis" is essentially the same as determining "how to develop a career in financial analysis." There is no straightforward answer to that question for a number of reasons. For example, such a question would force one to adhere to a vanilla-strategy approach and take for granted that students who are likely to become financial analysts simply settle into the role without even realizing it. Similarly, "How can I develop a career in financial analysis" assumes that those who become financial analysts are good at it, suggesting that anyone who isn't employed as a financial analyst simply did not find the industry.

However, what this section seeks to achieve is to determine what the right questions are to ask with respect to an industry that's transformed in drastic ways since the 2008 financial crash and yet acts as if nothing has changed. That is, most of the discussion in the prior portion of this paper reflects beliefs at banks and corporations with a distinctly Zen nature. Being accepted as a financial analyst is the same undertaking as becoming a member of a student organization. One will enter into that sphere when one is "ready" - that is, when one "really" believes in one's heart that one is already a member of the club. In other words, such a view presumes some 'sophisticated' ethos where recognizing the "right way" to build a career is simply not spoken of but simply understood on an intuitional or gut level. While scholars have made a bit of headway on the sorts of vocational and professional paths taken by investors with a buy-side focus, far less attention has been paid to career paths and networks for a financial analyst with sell-side focus.

Required Skills: Highly refined writing and communication skills are needed to ensure that technical data and analyses are clearly and explicitly laid out and comport with both the qualitative and quantitative analyses and the reasoning that underlies them. Quantitative skills to comprehend and calculate metrics, alongside the skill to comprehend the operational and legal consequences of financial results. Since smooth cooperation is needed to work with members in both operational fields and fellow team members in financial fields, social skills are required. Financial and economic concepts, information, procedures, accounting practices, and better comprehension that goes on to improve and augments the work are required. Trading, regulations, and personal relations are areas in which the analyst has to have extensive expertise. This is not formal or informal, as common perception would have it, in the sense of "Let's have lunch." "Let's talk about anything so that you'll come to understand me." Arcane or esoteric, not chit-chat. Rather, what is being discussed are industry and professional developments currently occurring. Talk about trading procedures, laws or regulations, roles, jobs, staff, bosses, tactics, strategies, and career movements. Why is it the firm is going in this or that direction? What is its short-term and long-term strategy for dominating or adapting to the market?

A. Skills and Qualifications

An expert in financial analysis is someone who is able to conduct a forensic investigation on the individual firm, such as a recent investment prospect that the investor intends to purchase, as well as the stock market in general. For example, the expert may not only analyze the individual financial statements of a firm, but she or he may also try to gauge the future of the U.S. stock market as well. For many individuals, the expert is also the person who selects and manages the professional investment managers who oversee the day-to-day investment activities of the retail investor and their respective portfolios. When you speak to people in the business world, they will often tell you that the ability to work with money and the ability to work in the world of finance is a "right brain, left brain" issue. What that means is that the left brain is the "business" side and requires a different level of intelligence than the right brain, which is the "math and number" side. In reality, there is some truth to the statement, but there are many sides to those statements as well.

Over the last several years, the world of finance and investing has grown far beyond the reach of even the most basic left- and right-brained computer systems. These changes show a dramatic rise in the level of intelligence required of a financial planner. The basic, or cardinal, skills that you will need if you want to succeed in the sphere of financial analysis include the following:

- Analytical skills: You need the ability to perceive and create clearer mental images. - Math skills: You need to be able to work through complex equations. - Pattern analysis: You need the ability to see numbers, trends, and the story behind those insights. - People skills: You need the ability to communicate clearly and concisely with a variety of people. - Tenacity: You must simply possess the drive and energy to work long, hard hours, as well as the ability to make decisions, adhere to problem-solving protocol, and make recommendations to existing and potential clients based upon fact.

To thrive in a successful career as a financial analyst, you must also possess the following:

- A solid, relevant education. - A strong skill foundation and current understanding of market changes. - A solid referral system and the ability to represent yourself with excellence.

B. Networking and Professional Growth
Networking and Professional Growth
Individuals forge connections and interact with colleagues both inside and outside of their companies through professional networks. These networks are composed of individuals moving toward shared professional, career, and often intellectual or academic goals. Networking forums take many forms, and successful business persons are often prolific networkers. Networking and professional involvement are particularly crucial in the international finance profession. By taking a leading part in professional networks, financial analysts help to establish their status as experts in their fields. They alert colleagues to their research and its promise, and demonstrate that they are conversant with and constructively supportive of the work of others. They are exposed to the ideas of others and can diffuse these ideas and serve as a mentor for their dissemination. It is important to select the networking choices that best suit the individual's professional and personal interests and are most supportive of the chosen career path.

Keeping an up-to-date resume, recording every important and successful conference paper and working project, and practicing frequently the development of a fifteen-minute informal biographical sketch are strategies to enhance skills in personal and professional networking. Having a professional biography or "bio" that is updated regularly is also a matter of preparedness. The ability to write a good bio enables one to have useful information available for use in many situations. It pays to have done the "homework" to create a well-written and engaging bio for a presentation or for use with a client, managing editor, or for an interview with a reporter looking for qualified personnel for a business story. Ideally, the financial analyst also has a professional web page or LinkedIn presence that can serve as a resource for the bio. In these contexts, "success" isn't just publication in top-tier international journals, it is contributions that lead to measurable improvements in research or decision-making practices in relevant organizations.

IX. Conclusion and Future Trends

The common thread running through all these very diverse papers is a focus on the needs of practicing (or soon-to-be-practicing) financial analysts, both buy- and sell-side. One could quite easily develop an extensive list of conclusions and implications that emerge from this concentration. The following, however, are probably those of greatest significance. We hope and trust that you will agree.

Investing success and adding value as an analyst, team member, and financial professional require deep knowledge of the company and industry in which you play a role. Those best able to analyze and understand are also those most likely to be effective in attracting and holding clients and/or investors. Understanding the tools and disciplines of financial professionals and the data to which they are based, at this level, significantly assists you to become a better analyst. Integration of views and focus on capital market ramifications add real value to insights. Be immersed in the facts, models, and hard numbers. All opinions must be based on assumptions of fact, not the other way around. Technology allows you to spend more time with coworkers, industry, and investors while also derisking your recommendations. Likely the emphasis will continue for expanding what is provided to sell-side analysts. They are the main source of earnings for most of the technology groups and are also deeply involved in the experiments of pedagogy in technology (and elsewhere). Expansion of materials on the buy-side is largely to further ensure that the resources of the OBRA will serve to close the practice-to-theory and practice-to-practice gaps. This, trained in the techniques currently employed by financial professionals, places a premium on accounting standards and other methods that are uniform, transparent, and helpful to the repayment of loans. Look for additional papers—and other materials—on the periodicity of reports, off-balance sheet financing, and value at risk as shown in the interest-rate swap debacle.

www.ingramcontent.com/pod-product-compliance
Lightning Source LLC
Chambersburg PA
CBHW051504140726

47987CB00006B/2874